Have You Ever Seen an Octopus with a Broom?

Written by Etta Kaner · Illustrated by Jeff Szuc

Kids Can Press

For Dr. Jane Goodall, who opened up
the world of animal tool use — E.K.

To all the animals of the world — J.S.

Text © 2009 Etta Kaner
Illustrations © 2009 Jeff Szuc

Kids Can Press acknowledges the financial support of the Government of
Ontario, through the Ontario Media Development Corporation's Ontario
Book Initiative; the Ontario Arts Council; the Canada Council for the Arts;
and the Government of Canada, through the BPIDP, for our publishing
activity.

Published in Canada by   Published in the U.S. by
Kids Can Press Ltd.   Kids Can Press Ltd.
29 Birch Avenue   2250 Military Road
Toronto, ON M4V 1E2   Tonawanda, NY 14150

www.kidscanpress.com

The artwork in this book was rendered in acrylic.
The text is set in Bodoni.

Edited by Karen Li
Designed by Marie Bartholomew
Printed and bound in China

This book is smyth sewn casebound.

CM 09 0 9 8 7 6 5 4 3 2 1

Library and Archives Canada Cataloguing in Publication
Kaner, Etta
   Have you ever seen an octopus with a broom? / Etta Kaner;
Jeff Szuc, illustrator.

(Have you ever seen)
For ages 4–7.
ISBN 978-1-55453-247-6 (bound)

1. Tool use in animals—Juvenile literature. I. Szuc, Jeff II. Title. III. Series.

QL49.K363 2009   j591.5   C2008-907559-5

Kids Can Press is a Corus™ Entertainment company

Contents

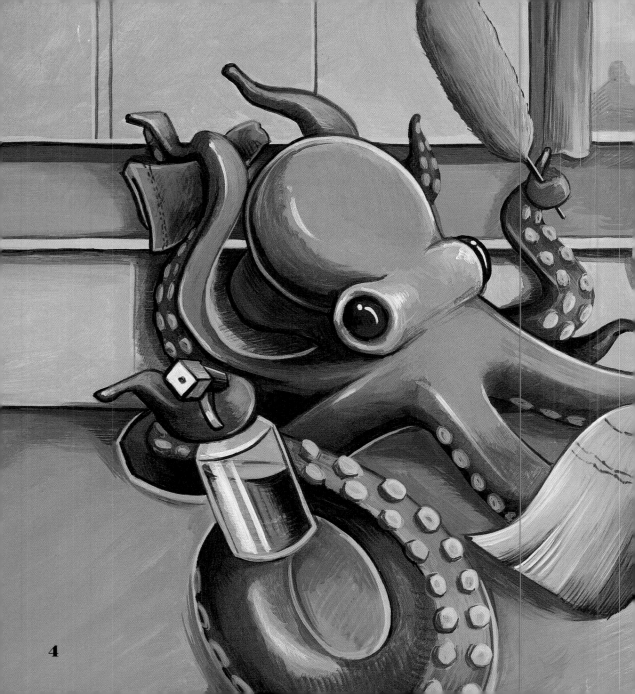

Have you ever seen
an octopus with a broom?

That's silly.

5

I clean our house with a broom.
Why would an octopus
need a broom?

6

An octopus cleans its house, too. It uses
water like a broom. After a meal, it pushes
leftovers out of its den with jets of water.
An octopus also sweeps sand and small
stones out of its den to make it bigger.

7

Have you ever seen a heron with a fishing rod?

8

That's silly.

I go fishing with a fishing rod.
Why would a heron need a fishing rod?

The green heron goes fishing, too. Its bait
might be an insect, a worm, a twig or a
berry. The heron drops the bait onto the
water and waits. When a fish swims up to
the bait, the heron grabs the fish with its
long pointed beak. Gulp!

11

Have you ever seen an ant with a shopping bag?

12

That's silly.

I carry food home in a shopping bag.
Why would an ant need a shopping bag?

An ant carries food home, too. Some ants use bits of leaves like shopping bags. They put the leaf bits on rotten fruit. The leaves soak up the fruit's juices. Then the ants carry the soaked leaves back to the nest. Ants can carry ten times more fruit juice this way.

Have you ever seen
a chimpanzee with a washcloth?

I clean my face and hands with a washcloth.
Why would a chimpanzee need a washcloth?

A chimpanzee cleans itself, too. It uses moss or leaves like a washcloth to wipe honey or fruit juices from its fur. A chimpanzee also uses moss or leaves like we use toilet paper.

19

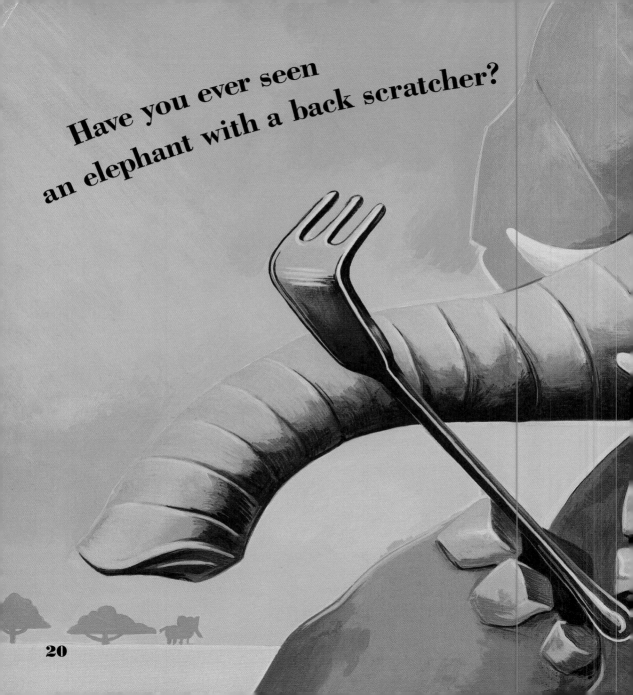

Have you ever seen
an elephant with a back scratcher?

That's silly.

21

An elephant scratches its back, too. It tears off a tree branch to use as a backscratcher. The elephant might even chew on one end of the branch or make the branch shorter to reach that itch. Aah, that feels good.

Have you ever seen
an otter with a nutcracker?

That's silly.

25

I crack open nutshells with a nutcracker.

Why would an otter need a nutcracker?

A sea otter cracks open shells, too. It opens the shells of clams and other shellfish. If the shell is very hard, the otter puts a flat rock on its chest. It smashes the shellfish on the rock until the shell breaks.

Have you ever seen
a cockatoo with a drum?

28

That's silly.

29

I play drums to make music.

Why would a cockatoo need a drum?

A palm cockatoo makes music, too. The cockatoo holds a stick in its claw and drums on a hollow log. At the same time, it whistles loudly and twirls around. It does all this to attract a mate.

Play Spin It!

Have you ever seen an animal play Spin It? Probably not. But you can play it! Here's how.

You will need

- a pencil
- a large paper clip
- a sheet of paper
- the game board inside the cover, or make a photocopy

1. The first player holds the paper clip with the point of the pencil in the circle. He spins the paper clip with his finger.

2. Wherever the paper clip stops, he must say up to two ways in which that animal is like a human or different. For example: (1) A heron is like a human because both catch fish. (2) A heron is different from a human because a heron has wings and a human has arms.

3. The next player follows the same rules. If she lands on the same animal, she may not repeat comparisons already given.

4. If a player can't think of a comparison, he may say "pass."

5. On the paper, keep a tally of the number of comparisons each player makes. The first player to make 12 comparisons wins. Good luck!